MISSION TO NIANGARA AND BACK

THE JOURNEY OF A SOUTHERN SUDANESE BOY TO MOBUTU'S CONGO TO BUY GUNS

Raphael Abiem

A Note from the Publisher

The publisher wishes to acknowledge and thank Dr Douglas H. Johnson for his invaluable help and support for Africa World Books and its mission of preserving and promoting African cultural and literary traditions and history. Dr Johnson and fellow historians have been instrumental in ensuring that African people remain connected to their past and their identity. Africa World Books is proud to carry on this mission.

© Raphael Abiem, 2020

ISBN: 978-0-6489698-2-2

All rights reserved. No part of this publication may be reproduced, stored in a retrieval system, or transmitted, in any form, or by any means, electronic, mechanical, photocopying, recording or otherwise, without the prior permission of the publishers.
This book is sold subject to the conditions that it shall not, by way of trade or otherwise, be lent, re-sold, hired out or otherwise circulated without the publisher's prior consent in any form of binding or cover other than in which it is published and without a similar condition including the condition being imposed on the subsequent purchaser.
Design and typesetting: Africa World Books

Contents

	Dedication	5
	Acknowledgement	7
I	United by Anger	9
II	Mission to Niangara	18
III	Niangara	23
IV	Lirangu	31
V	Attack on Lirangu Camp	34
VI	What Sank Adal?	40
VII	New Beginning, Same Struggle	47
	Notes	53

Dedication

This pamphlet is dedicated to the souls of Anya-Nya heroes (Southern Sudan's freedom movement from (1956 to 1972), those I was fortunate to have been with from 1965 to 66. Most of them have long since died, alas, unsung, and unremembered. My aim is to inject their memories into our current discourse and whatever discussions are afoot in the now independent South Sudan about honoring our veterans.

I would have achieved my goal were it only to serve as reminder that 'the now' in which we bask, stands on the shoulders of men and women long returned to dust. It is an invitation to be mindful of the grounds on which we stand; the more we know of, remember, and cherish this fact, the more confident we tread, not only on motherland, but also among the population on whose affairs we preside over.

Some of our departed heroes had led impactful lives for which they are remembered. Some are mentioned here, not with any depth from which additional knowledge could be gleaned. It is the slippery ones, those who did not live long enough to write their own stories, or have their stories widely told, if orally, that I attempt to beckon back to memory; they are one with the dust but it is on their remains we hoist the flag. It is them we offend with every act that defiles and undermines the spirit with which the struggle was conducted, the unity they forged out of a few frail ropes which tied southern ethnic groups together; it is they who, though limited by norther dominated and rationed education, negotiated with their feet the space on which subsequent movements, notably, the SPLA, stood grounds to launch the rebellion that has earned us the nation we call our own.

To memories of the unremembered, Ngeny, Ayok, Atar, Mayiel and Doldol and many more, may we all commit to keeping their candles alight.

For the living among my Anya-Nya friends, should you put your glasses on and read this piece, remember it is from an equally blurry of vision and tortured mind it flows. Memories tend to ebb away with time. I have tried to recover, best I could, of what I was able to retrieve from a distant past, fifty four years ago. To you who gave my childhood meaning and purpose, I say: Freedom remains my invaluable motto, my guiding star.

I caution readers, this work is an empirical account of contexts in which I was, people I had been with, activities I participated in and places I had been to. Nothing of historical value except when read as part of a bigger picture missing pieces to make it whole. We all know there is more to the story of Southern Sudan Liberation than "The Story".

*"Without Heroes, we are all plain people,
and don't know how far we can go."*
Bernard Malamud
1914-1986

Acknowledgement

A long silence, followed by plaudits in songs afterwards-a long while after the fact, is the Jieng way of acknowledging a favor well received. Generations would recite it, dance to its lyrics and tune, own and quote it; it is a shared cultural expression and a good legacy for the posterity of the acknowledged.

Alas, unless reclaimed, the back of Jieng culture is turned, grey and disappearing. But were my will to be done, it is in a song I would acknowledge Jacob Jiel Akol for his contribution to this pamphlet. But if there is no room for anachronisms, conventional English expression of appreciation would do.

To you, Jacob Jiel Akol, I say, were it not for your gentle prods, your insistence that I help populate the jigsaw, the largely untold story of the liberation of Southern Sudan, this pamphlet would not see the light. No one could have given me advice I would easily relate to than Jacob himself. In the 60's, we traversed the same bumpy road to the Congo, suffered comparable indignities there and emerged at the other end sobered by experiences.

One thing amazes me: how Jacob Jiel Akol awakened me to the realization it is a service to posterity to leave behind a trail showing the depth from which we come. Thank you. I am set to tell my story of how provocation to anger at an early age, though often sure to traumatize most children to incapacitation, also fuels others, catapults them to distances and paths they would otherwise never dream to traverse.

My gratitude also goes to Peter Lual Deng of Africa World Books Australia Publisher. One quiet morning, a mail delivery person rang the doorbell, asked me to sign on to a receipt, and off he went. It was a load of books authored by South Sudanese. I did not ask for them, did not pay for it; it was a surprise of a lifetime. Now that I think of it, the gesture was to awaken me to an obvious fact I did not pay attention to; time to share experiences about little known contributions to the struggle for South Sudan. I hope this modest effort, the story of a nine-year boy, will add to the overall picture of the struggle.

1

UNITED BY ANGER

It was on October 21st, 1964. The University of Khartoum Students Union, in a popular revolution, forced Ibrahim Abboud's led military junta to resign. Citizens were elated as they watched them blend in with oblivion's primary colors.

A stream of brilliant, western educated leaders stepped in to claim their share of the power pie. Some wore designer suits, even in the unforgiving heat of Khartoum; others, particularly those who traced roots to established religious homes, dressed in *jallabiya* (loose cloths), *immah* (turban) and pants.

Among these seemingly diehard traditionalists were graduates from Oxford, Cambridge, and Le Sorbonne, eager to bridge the yawning educational, perhaps spiritual gulf too, separating them from their political and religious bases. It was democracy cooking but, whether it would smell, taste, and feel to the touch like it when served, was for time to tell.

Doubts that matters would be as good-looking as the new men in charge persisted, especially among southern Sudanese, the segment of the population historically earmarked for raw experiences whenever changes occurred in the country.

But southern Sudanese misgivings aside, there was no denying the change had brought great jubilation to the country, one if handled well and anchored in good faith by leaders, all considered, could become contagious.

The August 18, 1955 rebellion had turned into a guerrilla warfare Abboud's regime tried to suppress but to no avail. The challenge facing his successor, Prime Minister, Sir-el-Katim el-Khalifa, was whether he would succeed where the military had failed. The proof of his success would be to honestly identify the root causes of the conflict and address them. That would end rebellion in southern Sudan.

Even southern Sudan, the odd region out, always the country's killing field, never a candidate for development, did momentarily experience some euphoria, though short lived as it would soon prove to be. As far away as El Nahud, a town in western Sudan where I attended elementary school, we sniffed the whiff of jubilation. We sang revolutionary songs the lyrics of which we did not understand.

The word, revolution, was in every man's, woman's, and child's mouth. Music was a big draw. It spoke in melody of a future free of civil wars and of discrimination based on race, region, or religion, (RRR), the evil trinity that had long threatened to break apart the largest landmass of any country in Africa. Our understanding of discrimination was modest and would demand modesty on the part of the new ruling elites to stoop to and resolve.

Southern Sudanese, especially those that did not know better, my type that was, knew out of experience we would be first to feel the impact of the new dispensation should things go wrong, as they easily did back then.

And so, we drifted along with our northern compatriots mimicking their slogans even when some phrases were regurgitations from the

Islamic tradition. We sang the national anthem *"Nahnu Jund Allah Jund Al-watan"*:

> We are Soldiers of God, Soldiers of homeland
> If called for redemption, we did not betray
> We challenge death upon ordeals
> We buy glory at most expensive price
> This land is ours
> May our Sudan live, an edifice among nations
> O Sons of the Sudan this is your symbol, carries
> The burden and protects your land"
> Composed by Ahmed Morjan in 1958 (1905-1974).

The song is much longer. Portions of it glorified a Sudan which was black and African: "We are black jungle sons, do not fear death or afraid of engagement." The author, Colonel Morjan, though born in Omdurman, had distinct African features even as he was consummately Arab in language and culture. Perhaps he entered this verse in honor of his ancestors who must have been descendants of some African tribe west, east, or south of the country

The lyrics were a reminder at long last, the people had regained their land and, therefore, their destiny. But I surmise it might as well have served to spice up the war in Southern Sudan as a fight between the soldiers of God and the forces of evil, a theological concept firmly implanted in faith and practice of Islam.

Regardless, the revolution was an occasion for southern Sudanese to blend in but cautious. Timely, the merry-filled moments would dim and set. We would return to our states of mind, firmly locked into our respective faiths, keen to defend our ethnic and cultural heritages. Our Muslim colleagues, by far the majority in school, would surely get back to what they did before the revolution: call us names such as "slaves" and "Firewood", a reference to hellfire prepared for non-Muslims who, themselves are the fuel of hell.

There was some truth to their abusive language. Truth was, our mothers, sisters and even some of us, school children, were servants in the homes of some of our richer northern colleagues. Sudan was socially stratified in such a way we thought that was the *status quo ante:* Uneducated Dinka people were servants in northern Arab homes; sanitation workers were from the Nubba Mountains. At sunset, these employees of the Ministry of Health, would walk from house to house, pick up pails filled with human feces from under dry toilets, and emptied the contents in sanitation trucks. As they labored unprotected not even by gloves and masks, jeering hordes of children ran after them shouting: "Neefa, Neefa, Neefa", that is, "putrid, putrid...".

Sudan ran a functional cast system without Hindu spirituality to explain and perhaps soften the bitter reality some people must suffer the lowly social status in life.

The Catholic missionary school we were in, Comboni, was mindful of our financial situation, so we were spared payment of back-breaking fees and did not have to work in the homes of our northern friends, at least not during the school year. The missionaries did their best to make us feel we belonged, but there were set boundaries they dared not cross: commitment to keep a strict divide between Muslims and Christians when it came to religious education. Lowering fence in this regard could easily arouse suspicions missionaries were intent on proselytizing Muslim children. That line was drawn in the sand, which they would not dare transgress.

A couple of years earlier, Abboud's regime had banished foreign missionaries in southern Sudan and had closed schools for the same reason. With that one act, Sudan arrested any semblance of progress in southern Sudan in terms of education. In response, young men joined Anya-Nya in their numbers, among them, Christopher Akonon Mithiang[1] from Abyei who became a prominent commander.

All that considered, southerners and northerners alike, heartily saluted the change. The acid test would be the degree to which the government would align rhetoric with policies and actions. If they erred on the side of use of force in southern Sudan, a strategy that did a great disservice to the military junta, right there would lie their doom. It was common knowledge, should government ignore the conflict burning at the southern edge of the country, they would have inadvertently made a rod for their own backs.

By mid-December 1964, jubilation had run its course. The ball was rolling fast towards conflict. School authorities realized instability had reached a point it looked unavoidable. Southerners in Khartoum had just had a violent brush with northerners due to rumors a prominent Southern politician, Clement Mboro, might have been lynched. Keeping us in school was growing by the minute a risk the school could not bear. We were sent back to Abyei[2]. We made it home safely. Dinka people who would attempt to come to Abyei through El Muglad after us, would not be as lucky as we had been.

January 1st, Sudan's Independence Day, passed uneventfully but ruling elites would soon reveal they were pseudo democrats who have long harbored racist views and attitudes towards southern Sudan and equally revolting, hate nurturing, religious and racial bigotry. Their public pronouncements made it abundantly clear they would do all they could to crash what they termed as: Christian missionary instigated conflict in southern Sudan. With their state of mind so set, the March 16, 1965 Round Table Conference was doomed to failure from inception.

The mask of affected respect for the people of Southern Sudan was lifted. Ruling elites no longer needed to suppress their innermost persuasion that they were Arab and Islamic. No more would they live ensnared between two opposed worldviews: the call to enlightenment, the function of received western education, and of hearts desirous to return to Arab and Islamic roots.

As the elites made no secret they would take after their forefathers, Southerners too, though unprepared, saw no alternative but to fish their way away from the north to find their own path if that were a jagged one. Disaster was in the offing.

The country was ineluctably plunging headlong into a war everyone was aware of, yet conveniently wished away. Then the news came from Western Sudan. Seasonal, labor-seeking Dinka farmers and home-helpers in and around the twin towns of Al Muglad and Babanusa, had been attacked. On that day, as laborers prepared to go to work to serve their masters/would be killers, they were rounded up, herded away in chains, and shoved into two large, grass-thatched police depots doused with Kerosene and…set alight. It was no news to whom that must have been a matter of grave concern, the authorities. Whatever had happened in Al Muglad and Babanusa, hardly sounded louder than a child's bursting soap bubble to the ruling elites. Yet, it was hundreds of men, women and children bursting in the conflagrations.

Ten years down the line, as a student in the University of Khartoum, Faculty of Law, I would find and delve into the archives and read perfunctory stories that appeared in the newspaper depicting scenes from that fateful day. Not one story carried a line that showed faint traces of sorrow for the victims. If anything, sardonic smiles (in script) littered the pages, punctuating the news items to highlight government's principled departure from soft approaches to ending war in the Sudan, to use of force.

Southern politicians understood the incident as a bait to lure them unprepared into reacting compulsively so violence could justifiably be unleashed. Suffice, the pain had registered but, grave as it was, hundreds of Dinka men, women and children killed, it was not inclusive enough to marshal southern Sudanese into unity. The good thing was, ruling elites were now exposed as autocratic to a fault, not the proponents of democratic ideals they have claimed all along.

Abyei was next in line to be cut down. Abyei is the administrative center of Ngok Dinka, approximately 10,547 miles in area; only 125 miles south of Al Muglad, the scene of massacres days earlier. Reportedly, a horde of well-armed men on horsebacks, backstopped by government forces, in a matter of hours, reduced the entire region to cinders.

The government was tight lipped. When pressed to speak, the refrain was, the incident was the result of tribal conflict, unavoidable when pastoralists rendezvous. Those were the kind of messages that went into historical records; statements to the contrary attracted no attention.

With Abyei incident also sure to go with the wind, the elites grew ever more confident they could, without consequences, continue playing ventriloquists behind northern characters in the killing fields. They were their cheer leaders, their financiers, and their voice to the outside world. Not once had government been held to account for their role, if not of directly masterminding the war, at least of ignoring it.

Distant observers of these genocidal attacks were Westerners on whom the elites had pulled tricks as mundane as dressing up in suits and painstakingly suppressing Arabic accent to sound more English… all in a bid to show they were worthy vessels for promotion of Western democratic virtues in the Sudan, perhaps Africa.

From the comfort of their exclusive ministerial villas in Khartoum, the 'Ten Homes', government ministers consumed the news capsules of intensifying attacks on southern Sudanese, in their homes and in northern cities. They did not see indiscriminate killings was quickly bringing south Sudanese together in increased cohesion among Anya-Nya fighting forces.

Then, the coordinated attacks on Juba, Wau and Malakal targeting intellectuals from all Southern ethnic backgrounds followed. More than 1700 were killed, 49 government officials. The southern newspaper, the Vigilant, on Sunday July 11, 1965, reported:

> Juba in Blood-Bath, Army Rounds Up Southern Civilians: Reports reaching here from Juba on Friday indicates that the army, the so-called security Forces of the Sudan Government went out in Juba town on what was described as "extermination operation mission" in the area.

All native quarters (Southerners) are reported to have been set on fire and over 200 (200) persons, all residents of Juba town who have never had any connection with Anya-Nya are reported to have been killed by the army and many more wounded, most of them, seriously.

This brought full awareness to southern Sudanese they were victims together. Southern Sudanese knew precious little about one another at the time, but they were provoked to anger together and so will they fight back as one. Northern Sudan had cast the dye for southern unity. I had already joined the rebellion but decided to return to the area to witness for myself the aftermath of Ngok's destruction. Abyei town was a no-go area; the population was homeless, squatting under trees south of Nyamoura River.

I was only nine years old, catapulted to adulthood by experiences. Many children were prematurely weaned of innocence; our eyes were heavily discolored by scenes of bloodshed and attracted to rebellion by the bitter experiences we endured. There was no need for pundits to explain to us what our eyes had seen: pure disregard for our lives.

Many years later, April 13, 1999, I would participate in a discussion panel organized by Yale law School. The topic was "Children in Combat: How Can We Protect Them?" The stated purpose of the event were: to raise awareness of the child soldiers issue within Yale community; to publicize the campaign going on at that time to stop the use of child soldiers, and to promote dialogue between students, NGOs, UN agencies and people directly involved in the field.

My interlocutor, a UNICEF official, was of the view all child soldiers in Africa were coerced to join the war. I saw some veracity in what she said, but I thought there was more to that. I had in my mind my own experience, which pointed otherwise. In my context, it was children, mostly those that saw the massacres, that pressured rebel leaders to carry them on their wings so they would grow into and contribute to the war of liberation in any way they could.

In my case, I needed a conduit through which I could express my anger at the gory spectacles to which I had been exposed. Anya-Nya, our rebel movement, availed me that opportunity, a decision I have not regretted.

The first Anya-Nya unit I joined was mono-ethnic, Dinka. The commander was Captain Minyang Apaie[3], from Panarou. One of his close adjutants was Lieutenant Macham Atem[4] from Twic Mayardit. Signs Southern Sudanese were uniting were beginning to show. We received[5], a Lotuka, into the unit; then Paul Mayiel[6], a Nuer, Moses[7], the trumpeter, a Ciec, and Alier[8], a Bor.

Alier said he was Dinka but, when he spoke, I had hard time figuring out what he was saying. He was heavily tattooed, a square man with a breast the width of a jeep track. He ported the one bran gun with a huge disk for a cartridge. One could put any load on him but that would not diminish his speed an inch.

I was still in my backyard watching Southern Sudanese mixing in real time. I saw the flower of unity bud, grow into fruit, ripen, and nourish the fledgling Anya-Nya Movement. Nothing could be more encouraging and wonderful to behold. Sharing suffering had earned us unity quicker than expected. I prayed leaders would find a way to maintain and even expand it into a vision that would transcend ethnic lines. Even as a child, I could understand the significance of more people from all backgrounds joining the movement.

I could also appreciate the importance of guarding this achievement because failing to maintain its purity would negate its utility, therefore, the weaker Southern Sudan would become.

I could not wait to see more of Southern Sudan, people, terrain forests, mountains, and animal life. In Abyei, the name Kur (stone) is commonplace, but not a pebble is seen in the soil. The first mountain I ever set eyes on was mountain Haidoub, in El Nahud. I could not wait to see more of its kind. Our mountains were anthills. If we wished to experience height, we climbed trees.

I wanted so much to be assigned to a serious mission that would take me far afield, to the deepest-most reaches of Southern Sudan.

II

Mission to Niangara

One morning, while attending routine rollcall, the commander of my new unit, Lieutenant Kuot Mayan[9], called out 17 of us for a special meeting. I said to myself whatever was held secret from older people, may prove too onerous for me to keep my mouth tight about. Then, I recalled, I was a corporal with two stripes, a superior to uncles whom I could command without thinking I was being impolite. I gathered courage and proceeded to where the meeting was to convene.

In the meeting, Lt. Kuot Mayan informed us that we were going on a long trip to Congo and that we would have a stopover in an Anya-Nya camp in Lirangu[10], a small town In Equatoria Province on the borders with the Congo. There, we would be instructed by Captain Nyiel Abot[11] and his Deputy, Fabio Deng Akol[12].

A question was raised how 17 of us, all Dinka, would pass through territories controlled by other ethnic groups and not expect attacks. We only had two rifles, one automatic gun and a limited supply of bullets. Captain Kuot assured us there was no cause for fear. He said, recent killings in Wau, Juba and Malakal in which educated sons from all ethnic groups were killed, had made Southern Sudanese realize we are one in this war. That sounded convincing. We were all set to go. I heard where we were supposed to travel to, but what that meant in terms of distance to cover, not a genius could have made me understand the implications involved in agreeing to brave the journey.

The next day, before the journey, Captain Kuot called me to his office (under a shade tree) and said my function in the journey would be to carry a small plastic bag he would tie on my back, attached to the skin. I inquired what it was, but he kept silent about it; so, I let the matter rest. He proceeded to tie the bag on me as he had told me. Now, I knew I truly counted as a soldier, not a tug-on, a burden to be tolerated on the way. I was kept in the dark about the bag yet pleased I had been honored with the assignment, whatever it took me.

I do not recall where exactly we camped when the journey started but it was somewhere in Rek area, a place I distinctly remember because of its white beach-like sands and lots of Doum Palm trees. Fruits of Doum tree, I have come to learn, contain a substance believed to be of therapeutic value in the treatment of bilharzia. It was there too that late Kerubino Kuanyin Bol[13], who later gained reputation as a fearless fighter if often a controversial one, joined our camp, his point of entry into the movement. He was closer to me in age, a bit older, but we had more in common. He came in a few days before we took off for the journey. I would visit him years later in the Presidential Palace in Khartoum, where he was assigned following Addis Ababa Accord that came into effect in 1972 which granted Southern Sudan a regional autonomy.

When we took the first steps away from the camp, I felt butterflies flap their powdery wings in my heart and stomach, preaching the gospel of fear of the unknown. But, when I remembered El Muglad/Babanusa massacres and the reduction of Abyei region to cinders, fear-preaching butterflies quickly got seared out of my system and consciousness about what I was here for dominated my thoughts throughout.

Our journey to the Congo was circuitous. Instead of travelling straight south to Zande land, from around Gagrial, we travelled towards Tonj. On the way, one attraction I cannot forget was the house of chief Aguer, Aguen Adel. I must confess his house was an aesthetics architectural marvel. Alas, I saw the building in an abandoned state. The vegetation had already encroached on it and had defaced some of its striking features.

We passed by Chief Aguer Adel's house. A short distance away, walked into a swath of wetland I thought would take no more than a couple of hours to cross. It turned out we were up against a much longer wading through the marshes. We walked and walked, from time to time, taking rest on small islands, then up for more ploughing.

When we emerged on the other end of the marshland, I was told we were in Agarland. I was thunderbolt to hear them speak Dinka. My reaction may have been ignorance on stilts, but still spoke to the truth Southern Sudanese knew precious little of one another; in some cases, downright dangerous lack of knowledge even within the same ethnic group as is the case with Ngok, my subtribe, and Agar. A few days later, we were in Commander Akonon Mithiang's camp.

We spent a few days there, then commenced our long journey west, past Wau, then south. In Rafili our guide led us straight into what would have been our assured death, a norther army barrack. We were a few feet away when we heard what sounded like a piece of cutlery fall on the floor, followed by a loud laughter. My cousin Ayok grabbed the guide and quickly muzzled him just in case it was his intent to lead us into the trap. One of our trip mates who, throughout the journey, suffered persistent cough, was mouth gagged as well till we were a safe distant away from the army camp.

We walked a mile or so in the bush, parallel to Wau/Tumbura road to Zandeland.

✣

I cannot recall how long it took us to arrive in Lirangu, but it was a journey as torturous as it was tortuous. It was a resilience test, but one I was pleased to have endured. Throughout our journey in the Zandeland, people were generous. In all villages we spent a night, we were directed to the house of the village chief who willingly shared with us what little food he had in store for his family.

On arrival to Lirangu, Lieutenant Kuot Mayan and I were called for a meeting to deliver the oddity he had tied on my back the day we embarked on the journey. It must have been an important something. I was instructed to sleep, swim, use the loo, whatever I did, it had to be on my back. My senior cousin, Ayok Dengabot[14], followed on my heels wherever I went, always armed with the only automatic rifle we had.

Was the bag the centerpiece for the journey? I wondered.

✣

I would feel relieved the sooner this tiny monstrosity came off my back; breeze would once again fan my back and life would return to normal. Soon, veteran politician, Elia Duang Arop[15]; Captain Nyiel Abot, Lirangu Camp Commander and his deputy, Fabio Deng Akol, walked in. I do not recall if Jacob Buok[16], an officer, and Robert Mayouk Deng[17], the two more senior colleagues whose company I enjoyed the most, were in attendance. This story would have been more complete had they informed the content as to the events that took place in Lirangu camp.

Now, the quorum was complete, and it was time to lay the burden down, a task accomplished. I was asked to stand up, so the bag is untied; it had gummed on me and had to be yanked off. A bit of my top skin went with it.

The bag was opened. A hefty bundle of cash, two thousand Sudanese Pounds, four US Dollars to one Sudanese Pound at that time, dropped on the table. It was the largest amount of cash I had ever seen. It was not South Sudan of today. Money was a rarity we saw circulating in the hands of Arab merchants. If it trickled down to the hands of Southerners, it was pittance.

But what was the money for, I still wanted to know? Lieutenant Kuot Mayan later confided in me that the money was earmarked for purchase of weapons in the Congo. The Simba, a Congolese 'liberation movement', had been defeated and weapons were reportedly in abundance for sale. He patted me on the back saying, "you are a valued member of the team tasked to accomplish this purpose". I felt uplifted and looked forward for that day of the great transaction.

III

NIANGARA

We stayed in Lirangu for almost two weeks, then, continued the journey to Niangara, a Northern Congolese town on the Uele River, the northern region of Haut-Uele. We arrived on January 1, 1966. It was weekend, so we could not meet with Major Thomas Dhol Theil[18] as was instructed in Lirangu. Niangara[19] was clearly a town reeling under the thumb of a lingering war. It was recaptured from Simba rebels in April 1965 by soldiers of fortune (mercenaries) hired by 'Moboutu' Sese Seko, full name: *"Moboutu Sese Seko Ngbendu Wa Za Banga"* to fight the war on his government's behalf.

We were told Niangara was a silhouette of what it was. But even as it stood, a ghost of her former self, one could see it was once a small town with a future. Deep trauma had driven the population to life, if life it was, on the edge. Scars of war were on the faces of the few brick buildings strong enough to endure and stand testimony to turbulences the town had been through.

So, buildings too could tell stories? I muttered to myself. I recalled when Abyei region was burned down, not a brick was there to speak for the magnitude of disaster that had befallen unsuspecting communities. It was cows culled, agricultural produce burned, people murdered and buried and grass thatched homes with mud walls, burned down. One rainfall and evidence was gone. With earth leveled, nothing was left to see but a land that spoke of no atrocities committed. No solid structures were there to bear witness.

But what would all this add up to when reporting conflicts in impoverished communities? Unlike Niangara, in Abyei, only graves of human beings killed stood as evidence; nothing else was there to corroborate claims of extensive losses, human and material. On hindsight, I know now wars are often remembered, less about human casualties, and more about material losses sustained. Abyei has never had a solid face which, when scratched, would endure to bear witness to what had happened. It has many times been leveled to the ground but, every time that happened, there was not much evidence left standing, if damaged, to make the news.

Niangara was poor. It had one main street and a few solid structures. That one main street was packed with mercenaries' Congolese people with trembling knees, referred to in hashed tones, "Belgians". They ran loose in town looting, imposing order while drunk and chaotic as the traumatized population they sought to control. They roamed backstreets too; along their path, kicked the living and the dead alike; stopped to dally and kiss women they fancied and despised in one breath; shot to death any Simba lookalike mixed with the population. In a word, the entire population of Niangara, in fact, Haut Uele Province in general was to them, suspects and fair game to kill. Nothing differentiated Simba affiliates from the rest of the population as they all hailed from the region and from all northern ethnic groups. Simply, mercenaries were trigger crazed dogs of war itching to shoot. Uele River was there to receive the dead, a graveyard of convenience.

Niangara

We had a rough night. The days that followed would not be any calmer, a fact of life we could not avoid.

The next day, we met with Major Thomas Dhel Thiel. He told me to join a local missionary school immediately. I did not like what I heard. Despite my reluctance, several days later, commander Dhel would take me to school anyway. Undoubtedly, that was a show of good intention on his part which, politely, I turn downed. My reason, as always was, I did not rebel to join school in another country but to contribute to efforts aiming at restoring the dignity of my people. I gave it a try, just in case.

In class, I could not understand a word. Teachers jived as they taught. Children took to dancing with every word and move he made. Were they hearing music so subtle I could not hear? I felt straight jacketed; a captive audience among children I thought were borne dancing freaks. I knew even I were to endure classes taught in Lingala and French, still I would not be able to understand their way of life. I could not see a sliver of silver lining in Major Thomas Dhel's advice even as those were the reasonable advice any concerned relative would give a child. But no. I had cast the 'reasoning key' in Nyamoura River when I left Abyei. My mind was locked into the struggle at hand. Four days later, I abandoned school, a definitive rejection of my superiors' advice.

With talk about school out of the way, my mind quickly turned to the initial assignment: purchase of arms, a topic everyone had recently been skittish about since the day the money bag was taken off my back. I looked for clues in the eyes of my superiors' not a bite worth information was discernible.

Was that corruption at work, I wondered? No! Who the cursed would have known such a word back in southern Sudan of the 60's, let alone practice it? Unthinkable. We still feared the *Most High*. He was living among us, not the transcendent God theologians have made Him out to be. Also, our ancestors were evermore present in spirit, seated in large rooms with their backs rested against the walls watching every move we made and apportioning curses or blessings according to our deeds. Totems were witnesses even in their holes. And so, to be moral was not to moralize; it was life lived with consequences, good or bad. We feared the unknown more than clear and present danger that man presents. Conscience never went to sleep. It had to throb at the pace of heartbeats, poised to censor deleterious thoughts which, left untrimmed, would mushroom into the kind of bushes under which corruption evil vine would grow. Not a soul was so lost as to deviate in that way.

Was the silence then a function of utmost secrecy? I hoped that was the case. If it were, I would still see the results, if not here in the Congo, then in Lirangu upon return. I could not hide my frustration but decided not to broach a word till we were back home in southern Sudan

❂

We spent a month in Niangara. Food was scarce. A small shack near our residence doubled as somebody's bedroom by night and a restaurant by day. Fish was served at four in the evening, a perfect timing. We could afford one meal a day, which was good enough, especially when we did not have to walk distances to find food in a town thronged with death-disbursing mercenaries.

One day, we had barely been through our usual meal when I picked a strange object in the fish. It felt to the touch like fish scale only harder. I stopped eating to have a close look at it. I could not figure out what it was or, perhaps, I was reluctant to accept what I saw, was what I had in mind. I passed it on to Lieutenant Kuot Mayan who cast a look at it and mattered in muted, dignified voice: "it is human nail". We pushed the dish aside, still famished, of course, but nauseated at the thought we were one degree removed from cannibalism. We should have known there were too many dead bodies thrown into Uele River every day; that was surely food for fish. I felt living any longer in Niangara was to volunteer for early death for no worthy cause. In my case, nothing other than the cause for which I had to bear the rigors of the journey would make me embrace danger.

I longed to get back to the Sudan to fight my war, even if with bare hands. Returning home with weapons at hand was worth the hunger I had to endure, and the distances I had to walk. Nothing deserved the sacrifice but the liberation of my people from suppression.

The one month we spent in Niangara, other than watching horror in real time and places, it was overall uneventful. Food was scarce now that fish was a scare. For change, I thought I should take a second look at Niangara. Perhaps I would see a thing or two that would impart some color to the bleak portrait I had in mind, a saving grace for Niangara. I decided to take a short stroll around the block of homes where I lived right on Uele River but hoped I would not catch sight of fish or anything that swam or floated. Just in case, my senses were on full alert ready to delete anything that looked like an aquatic creature. I wanted to appreciate the water which ran crystal clear; dotting the water stream were sparsely paced brown rocks, clean shaved by frothy waves.

On hindsight, now that my eyes have been influenced by close contacts with affluence, I imagined the rocks would be ideal spots for reflection when the town would be safe and people sane enough to think beyond finding food and alcohol.

After some time, I snapped out of my daydreaming, looked around; not a soul was there. I was alone engrossed in unrealistic imagination of the river's potential. Adorned in shades of blue and frothy white, Uele River sped on as if dancing on a long theatre dotted with rocks. It was a wonderful sight for me, a denizen of a region right on the mouth of a devouring desertification. Perhaps not many eyes in Niangara were clear enough to watch the waves gently cat-walk on the rocks as if performing ritualistic cleansing rites waiting for the day Niangara would shake off bad habits, if habits we saw play out, and rise in glory to transform the banks of Uele River into a sight to marvel about.

I could not help sigh in desperation when my thoughts suddenly dashed off to Abyei, my homeland and started wondering, will there ever be hope? I found no room for comparison between Abyei, an arid region, and Haut-Uele, a region, if tittering at the brink of destruction and self-mutilation, still was home to nature. I would not allow my mind to float too long in that direction for fear of conjuring hopes that neither history, nor reasonable prognostication of Abyei's checkered past and threatened future, would confirm.

Instead, I focused more on the nature of the two regions, to show why Niangara appeared attractive despite the gory experiences outlined elsewhere in the story. The magic was in Niangara's sky and her lifeline, the Uele River, both of which spoke of abundance waiting for future intentional generations of Congolese to harvest. But for now, layers of confusing events have blinded that generation of Congolese from seeing Niangara for what it was and will be, a gift of nature.

Abyei was another story altogether; not that nature was particularly repressive, if indeed it often had been, but because of its location in Africa, the line separating Africans from self-confessed Arab tribes whose life vocation is to covet territories long inhabited by African tribes. Wherever the hooves of their horses stepped, that was the seal they needed to authenticate claims to territories and the right of might was there to back that up.

Abyei's conflict was not and still is not rooted in the mindset of a few evanescent politicians sworn to self-enrich as was the case in the Congo and dogs of war during Mobuto Se Seko regime; it is systemic, rested on political, historical, cultural, and religious depths passed on with varied intensity, from generation to generation; it is a conflict more involved and its dimensions extend well beyond the borders of the Sudan.

Arab tribes did and still do launch proxy raids today backed up by all manner of governments that have ruled the Sudan: dictatorships, democracies, oppressive democracies, and theocracies. Their mission, if not stated, has been to cyclically disrupt life in indigenous, African communities, Abyei region being one. It has been invaded many times and threats of full-scale invasion remain true.

Musing along Uele River took me a while but finally jolted back to consciousness only to find I was on the banks of Uele River; still in Niangara, in the Congo, a thousand Kilometer away from Abyei and from her ill-hydrated river, Nyamoura or, *Bhar el Arab*, as Arabs have come to name it in advance of owning it. I had drunk to the fill with my own brew of make-believe peace and lived the illusion I walked on safe shores. But no, I was a few steps away from where I had witnessed many indescribable acts of brutality, the very spot I saw the starved drop dead; diseases ravage communities and white armed men, brandish gadgets of destruction and merrily going about warning the population of more death to come.

Uele River was the true host of Niangara; though much desecrated, it has remained a source of food for the living and resting ground for the dead. For the length of time I spent there, it was with her I communed when I was enraged and frustrated by vanishing hope, we would ever honor the purpose for which we journeyed to the Congo. It is her I went for audience when fear stricken or chocked with anger about abuses taking place in the neighborhood with no one held answerable. Uele River was my therapist and trusted confidant. I whispered my innermost concerns, and even worries about how Southern Sudanese would fend for themselves when aggressed from the north. I felt she could hear me out.

When it was time to leave Niangara for Southern Sudan, I was fully reconciled with the Congo, and with Niangara, town and region. Then, one last attraction to remember Niangara for, a row of women with elongated heads, I mean long, backward pointing heads, passed by. I was told they were members of an ethic group called, the Mangbetu, indigenous to Haut Uele Province, home to many other ethnic groups including the Zande.

Mangbetu people believe beauty must be enhanced by human

ingenuity. Mothers would not trust nature or genes to determine how their daughters would look in adulthood. From infancy, a girl's head is tightly wrapped in clothes, so it elongates, the longer the head, the more beautiful in the mother's eyes and perhaps, society at large. Today, I wonder what rights groups would make of such cultural practice. Would it count as another form of human rights abuse comparable to female genital mutilation, or would it be praised as was the practice of tight lacing in which 18th century European women were pressured to wear tight corsets for modified esthetic appearance?

On this note, I bid goodbye to Niangara, a town I hated, then feared and finally loved; a town whose defining feature, River Uele, was my special counselor who spoke in tongues and sometimes roared, yet I could understand. When I was at the end of my tether in patience with my comrades, my kin, and kith, it was Uele I turned to for wisdom.

IV

LIRANGU

We left Niangara on the first week of February 1966, or thereabout, for Lirangu. The enthusiasm that fueled my tiny body to endure a journey of over 980 km, had ebbed away. My knees were weak. I remembered the biblical story of Samson, how he lost his hair, the source of his power, to a beguiling woman, Delilah who, in the end, handed him over into the hands of his enemies.

The parallel was vivid in my mind. Had I been beguiled too by my kinsmen who brought me this far only to line my eyes with more scenes of human suffering? I remembered the source from which I drew stamina to withstand the perils of the journey: hunger, diseases, life threatening encounters and fear of the unknown. All that was worth enduring if the outcome would be to shake free of oppression. When I learned the money which I carried on my back was for the purchase of weapons, I was ecstatic, and filled with power. I regretted not one step of the nearly one thousand Kilometer I walked to the

Congo. That was my source of power. Whoever took that spirit away had robed me of my all. That person was my Delilah.

Now that incentive seemed to have been taken away, I saw no difference being here or there. I fervently prayed my seniors had secretly done the right thing without informing me. I did not have much else to think about or live for. My thoughts shuttled between frustration and artless anticipation. If only I had a choice, I would have stood still in my footsteps and refuse to continue a journey I felt was without purpose or destination. Here, the spot in which I stood, was closer to Niangara where weapons should have been purchased. A step further away north felt like abandonment of a solemn undertaking. Never had a journey been so long and yet so fruitless. Meanwhile, the cause for which we walked this far stood evermore threatened.

Finally, we arrived at Lirangu. Throughout the journey, I was drowned in my thoughts and could not spare a thought to check who my road companions were but Lieutenant Kuot Mayan, the only one to whom I turned for avuncular advice.

Lirangu is a town in Western Equatoria region, home to the Zande ethnic group, part of which is indigenous to the Congo's Haut Uele Province and to the eastern region of Central African Republic. It was built around a Leprosy hospital, perhaps the only specialized hospital of its kind in Southern Sudan at that time. Most buildings were made of red bricks, designed, and built during the British colonial administration. When civil war spread to all areas of Southern Sudan, Lirangu hospital was among many facilities that were abandoned.

By 1965, Lirangu had been reclaimed by thick, forbidding jungle only a few would dare casually venture into. It was there, some distance north of Lirangu ruins, that Anya-Nya set up a camp which looked a little Dinka colony but for the fact that they were there as freedom fighters.

Zande people were accommodating and even generous with the little resources they had at hand. The news Arabs were at war with all the peoples of Southern Sudan, apparently left no room for tribalism. If they harbored thoughts to the contrary, they were concealed; and if at all they had reservations, from all indications, it was nothing they could not tolerate.

I did not understand a word of the Zande language (Pazande), but when I heard it spoken, sentences invariably ended with comforting melodic notes. For instance, "How are you?" *Gini pai* in Pazande, when pronounced, rings musical. It was in Zandeland I saw, for the first time, musical instruments such as harps, mandolin, *sanza*, and more, all locally handcrafted. Zande people are also skilled in woodcarving; their music is multipurpose. It expresses joy, sadness, and a system to alert villages of approaching dangers.

Zande people were the human custodians of Lirangu, but mother-nature was the hands-on owner. For years, it had silently been demolishing what remained of man's handiwork and, instead, planted trees and flowers of her choice. She was the uncontested protector too. In her hands, Anya-Nya set up a camp, walled in by fruit trees including mango, orange, tangerine, banana, pineapple, and oil palm, all mother-nature's gift. Anya-Nya could not have camped in a safer place nor among more accommodating people. The camp was difficult to access even by inhabitants of nearby villages.

V

Attack on Lirangu Camp

Yambio and Nzara, the nearest Northern army garrisons from which danger could come, posed no danger. The forest was too thick for any aggressor to venture into. The sense of security in the camp was such that it could easily slip into complacency. Writing was on trees and leaves but indecipherable to human eye. Security was lax. All considered, Lirangu appeared a haven walled in by the hands of nature. Life in the camp was secure but a humdrum.

Food was served twice a day. Sometimes, we took hikes in the wild to gather fruits. I do not recall how and from where other kinds of food were sourced, but judging from the way Zande people were receptive of our presence, to show solidarity, they must have shared their food with us.

Other than eating, exercising, and attending roll calls twice a day, there was not much to do in the camp. There was no ideology to discuss, no ambitions, besides fighting the war, to pursue and no identified skills to hone. Attending weekly market days held on Thursdays was our only source of entertainment. Even that was strictly regulated. On market days, nearby villages gathered in one location to barter or sell their goods. It was there we had a chance to meet and learn from Zande people about their way of life.

Inside the camp, we spent time telling narratives of close encounters with death and other tales of valor. Our camp was all Dinka, so we told Dinka tales but precious little about the movement, its present and future challenges, especially how to consolidate unity across southern Sudanese. From what I heard, most Anya-Nya camps were like ours, not sufficiently mixed to warrant the conclusion and a sigh of relief: at long last, our unity pot was melting. If anything, in some ways, each Anya-Nya camp remained fiercely autonomous. A step on a community's toe could ruin all efforts at forging understanding across ethnic lines and dwarf the idea, "as we suffered together, so must we strife together".

Lirangu was not only home to gigantic trees and beautiful, giving, and protective nature. There were also mean-spirited, tiny freaks of nature, parasites, and other insects, worse among them a worm the Zande people call *Tukutuku*. Elsewhere in the world it is called jigger or *Tunga penetrans*. They are tiny worms that penetrate under the toenails and silently suck blood. When it is fully grown, it is the size of a chickpea. My toes are a living testimony to how treacherous *Tukutuku* can be. In some cases, infection becomes so severe toes must be amputated, an irreversible disfigurement.

There are reports *Tukutuk* was "inadvertently introduced by humans into sub-Saharan Africa" from Central and South America where it is indigenous. This may lend credence to claims Africa has been a victim, not only of invading cultures, but also of parasitic humans such as we met in Niangara.

February sped by, then March. With every passing day, my anxiety mounted. I expected a cache of arms to be handed out anytime during one of the roll calls to those old enough to bear them. But from the way things looked, we were in Lirangu for a long haul. A day in was as good as another just gone. We expected endless days to come our way off God's inexhaustible calendar days.

April, I have come to learn from other cultures, is a month that starts with lies. That night, an April date I cannot recall, must have been the trick night. It created an illusion all was normal; that peace was the inviolable rule, and that exceptions did not happen in the jungles of Lirangu. Our minds were at rest. The combination of lunar influence and April allure had done us in, and we did not know, not till it was too late. With the tempo and monotony of grandfather's clock, unconcerned, we watched days silently peel off the calendar. Amidst this mirage of tranquility, my mind was tempestuous, disturbed about continued lack of armaments with which to defend ourselves in case there were attacks.

One day, I accompanied an older colleague to one market day event in the abandoned ruins of Lirangu. It was a good experience. Items on sale included palm wine, palm oil, plantains, ground peanuts and assortment of bush meats, including monkey meat.

As we were returning to the camp, in the ruins of Lirangu hospital, my colleague asked me to momentarily take custody of his China-made, semi-automatic gun so he could step into the privacy of the ruins to relieve himself. He instructed me to be alert, place my finger on the trigger, but never pull unless there was danger, all of which I committed to heart, perhaps a bit too much. My eyes dilated; my mind, throbbed, geared on high alert, scanning for any danger lurking in the woods, or hidden behind piles of bricks unplugged by bulldozing roots. It was as if the weapons I had dreamed about were in my custody; no, in the palms of my hand. No more fear enemies would attack and flee unharmed.

I was engrossed in another dream, a pleasant one. Suddenly, a loud bang! I had inadvertently pulled the trigger, scaring off serenity of the environment and of my colleague too, who, in a jiffy, appeared from behind the bushes, ash-white with fear. When he noticed it was false alarm, fear gave way to murderous anger. I could feel it as we walked back to the camp.

We arrived on time for the roll call. The commanding officer asked if there were anything to report. My companion stepped forward and narrated the incident. He had to, because, at some point, he would have to account for the missing bullet. Before roll call was dismissed, the camp commander, Captain Nyiel Abot, asked me to step forward. Ceremoniously, he demoted me to a private from corporal and ordered me detained.

When we arrived at the detention center, I was hand and foot tied. I do not recall how long the detention was supposed to last. But something singularly detestable would soon send us back to *Bhar el Ghazal Province* unprepared.

The camp had three entry points: North, East and South gates. I was tied up and detained in the South Gate, the entry-point most guarded as it was also most exposed. The eastern gate was the entrance to the senior officers' quarters. There, Commander Nyiel Abot and his deputy, Fabio Deng Akol, lived. I do not know who else lived with them.

Night hours were growing larger and closer to retirement. Waiting for the clock to strike 12, were new guards come to hold vigil till daybreak. It was one o'clock AM… two…three…. Daytime was approaching, but not quite yet. Human mind was at it once again, cutting corners in a bid to self-assure all was working out to his expectation, the usual break in of another day. But what transpired in that serine night made me realize later in life, human beings always walk into the future, remote or proximate, blindfolded. They seem not to understand how an object so close and easily attainable would still be beyond reach if still rested in the hands of time future. That, between a minute and another or here and there, lies eternity packed with undetectable possibilities, still elude human attention.

That tantalizing early April morning stands testimony to the truth nothing is in the grip of man which destiny cannot seize and walk away with.

It was four o'clock. The moon shone silvery bright, the brightest I have ever seen. Years later, because of what happened that morning, I could almost appreciate the rational why other cultures have come to celebrate the "April Day of Fools". To me, against the backdrop of my experience that morning, April was, "The month that fools". It fooled us with a night so beautiful in the wild, yet romantic in her stillness. Suddenly, it turned murderous. Ho..., I could not pronounce the third letter. Bang...crack...crack...pow...pow. We were under attack from the eastern gate where senior officers lived.

The guards at the Southern Gate, where I was detained, immediately fled upon hearing gunshots, leaving me hands and feet tied. I was on my own, waiting for what was in store for me. It was here; yet there; may be, never; all was in future. April had beguiled us with beauty to serve us death. I heard footsteps. Whatever I was waiting for was here. Until it befell me, I would not know. If death were fellow human, it would be a cat footed thief.

It was a Zande man running west for his life. He saw me and stopped, not minding a minute lost could cost him his life. For what reason, I asked myself, would he, a Zande, stop to rescue me, a boy, a Dinka for that matter? That was a foolish soliloquy; the man was a human being before incarnation to a Zande tribesman. It was from him I learned tribalism is a synthetic thought pattern. It is learned, can be challenged, and if not rooted in reason, trashed as will all things manmade when they lose appeal.

The man untied me quickly and ran his way westward. I followed in his path. I knew I had to run opposite the direction of the shooting. I could not run north because I would pass through the main camp which, by then, would have been occupied by government troops. I was not informed of the secret code of the night as detainees are not supposed to be privy to such sensitive information. Perfectly clueless of where I was heading to, I kept on running west. After an hour, I veered a little to the north in hope I would find a freshly beaten footpath. I walked for half hour more, then veered right; in a zigzag till, luck struck.

I found my people gathered, counting the present, and taking note of the missing, prominent among them, the camp commander, Edward Nyiel Abot and his deputy, Fabio Deng Akol. By the end of the day, only the two never resurfaced. They were marked missing or dead.

I do not recall attempts to verify whether they were indeed killed there and then or, perhaps, captured alive, interrogated, and then killed. That detail, I reckon, may never be known. I still cringe at the thought of walking away leaving their remains for the elements to dispose of; but we did, not out of cruelty, but because we had no arms to strike back with. The thought they were never given a befitting burial, weighed heavily in my heart, but we had to move on.

That was how our journey back to Bhar-el-Ghazal Province started. We did not plan for it.

VI

What Sank Adhal?

The first hours were a litany of profound doubts. I felt discouraged and overwhelmed by incidents that dropped on us unprepared. We all wore long weary faces and changed countenances. As more silence prevailed, disheartening thoughts filled in the vacuum making us appear more miserable and disoriented. We sat under trees with scattered minds, heavy hearts, and foggy eyes waiting for an epiphany, something to cast light on the direction and path we should take. With the commander and his deputy gone and no obvious person to take the lead, every step any direction was a serious undertaking.

My mind flashed back on our trip to Lirangu. We had guides that were intimately familiar with both the topography of Bahr el Ghazal and Western Equatoria: mountains, rivers, towns, and villages along the way and yet they made mistakes that could have been fatal. We followed paths that were not frequently patrolled by government army. Knowing we were too ill-prepared to assume unnecessary risks, we avoided sauntering into roads and villages we knew nothing about; my fear was we did not have someone as familiar with the terrain to guide us through. Water streams presented a danger from which we had to steer clear. Some were infested with dangerous creatures: crocodiles, hippopotami, pythons and even turtles large enough to pose risks to human beings.

I had no idea what thoughts passed through other people's minds as we waited. With no blanket to slip into, I sank deep into my thoughts, regurgitating horrors that had whizzed me off to far flung lands and destinations; and now, here under the foot of a gigantic tree. Who knows how long it would be before we figured out when, how and where to go? I felt empty and gutted; my will, my wheels, as it were, was flat. Should I resign and wait for what comes as I had to this early morning, I said to myself? If such were the choice, then here I rust, fragment, and be one with the soil.

I would not have hit this low point had it only been for that morning attack and the great losses we incurred. I knew, firsthand, in war, people get killed. However, to choose to fight without weapons, even when there were opportunities to acquire them, was what robbed me of the spirit, the driving force behind my decision to join the movement in the first place.

In a state of delirium, I soliloquized and expressed myself to my satisfaction, but when asked questions, I could not speak coherently. I must have appeared to my companions as deeply asleep, so they left me to my musings under a tree I seemed to have hogged all to myself.

A boy my age, one with eyes so wide he could see nothing, barged in, and punctuated my horrid day time dream. He spoke down at me, admonishing me for failing to see what he described as, the "big picture", the reality of liberation struggles.

"Up on your feet; continue the journey north", he said in a firm voice. I was convinced he had no clue why we were here under these trees. Annoyed, I answered back: "walk away and leave behind the remains of our leaders? Walk away and confirm, in this unarmed movement, our duty was to sacrifice the ultimate yet remain persuaded that, somehow, victory was ours?"

In a moment of sincerity, I could see myself in him a year ago following Abyei's incineration. I was then upbeat, younger, enthusiastic, and mindlessly daring and, truly angry. I felt I was forged and tested by gory experiences in northern, southern Sudan, and a year of travails on the long meandering road to the Congo, Niangara town.

The more I engaged him, the more this young apparition hammered lessons into my sleepy ears and listless soul. I told him I was typical '*him*' a year ago, but post Niangara, due to successive disappointments I have not been the same person.

He paid a deaf year to what I said and proceeded: "wise up; overcome your frustrations and say to yourself, nothing is lost. When death and suffering are met with strong determination, future bends and allows itself to be shaped."

In my heart, I chuckled, "what a little brat he must be to even think, let alone believe, future would bend for humans to shape"! I asked, "How would you explain this morning's incident, was it that we did not do enough to influence the course nature should take?"

He noticed I was unhappy with his sweeping, idealistic remarks. He continued to rain down advice after advice even as I drooled in that state of pitiful indolence: "Remember", he continued, "future is as much a giver as it is a taker. This morning, it took the best of us; in exchange, gave us anger, frustration, and inanition. Were these not the very feelings you had in Abyei when you decided to shed the child in you and, overnight, became a freedom fighter? The weights such as we carry this morning, are what would create the resolve needed to take charge of our destiny, which is now firmly rested in the palms of the government in Khartoum." Then as if he never were, vanished.

At that moment, a bee stung me on the right cheek. I wondered if that were my muse's way of ending the conversation, with an awakening pinch that temporarily slammed my mouth shut till our path home was found.

What Sank Adhal?

Whoever the bee was an emissary for, the task to discipline me was accomplished with excellence. That would be my last time to yield to energy sapping musings. I swore I would face up to all challenges along the way. Unlike trees which cannot help themselves even as loggers clear neighboring trees, human beings are blessed with the power of mobility, the first act of self-defense. As refugees and freedom fighters would say: we voted with our feet, therefore, we are today. The 800-mile journey we were about to embark on, would no doubt count as a line in the records of the liberation struggle.

At about four that afternoon, we were asked to stand in line and be counted. We did. It was announced, in half hour, we would be on our way. We rushed to our trees to collect whatever belongings we had. I had none but the rags on me. My feet were bare and perfectly exposed to elements, the most dreaded of which was the tiny man eaters, toenails nemeses, the *tukutuku*.

Lirangu is located north of Yambio/north east of Nzara. The forces that attacked our camp may have come from either town, but most likely from Nzara. As mentioned above, much as we needed to pass through villages to purchase food supplies, it was wiser to stick to the jungle tracts and avoid walking along riversides. There were no indications the Zande people would betray us, but it was necessary to exercise caution. From where we left, we headed north making sure we avoided human habitats. We straddled the path between the Sue River (River Bhar el Ghazal) to the west and Ibba River (Tonj River), to the east.

We walked for days, eating off the bounties of nature: wild honey, availing ourselves of fresh animal meat; now and then, we would run into small creeks teeming with fish, some, species I had not seen before. But again, everything about Western Equatoria was mystery to me. Nature was colorful. Yesterday it was grassland shooting up to a height of 15 feet; then, as if to give us a short respite before encounter with even more stifling surprise, suddenly, a clear parcel of land appears. The mind is cleared, the heart pulsates at a normal rate, and nature is less intimidating.

The short grass suddenly yielded as we entered probably the thickest, least explored area in the southern region, the great forest Dinka people call *Roor Chol Akol* which, translated, would mean, the forest in which the sun gets dark. Perhaps that is a metaphor for trees growing so tall they could block sunlight for days. The British called it, the Southern National Park. In the fifties and earlier, the British employed guards to regulate entrance into the forest, especially by non-natives to the environment. There were even rest houses for tourists 150 Kilometer North of Yambio at the edge of the Zande side of the park before entry into Tonj, Bhar el Ghazal region. A road paved for that purpose extended from Yambio to the park.

Animal life was beyond my wildest expectations. They gather in large numbers in locations, I have come to learn, were salt licks where animals, particularly larger ones: buffalos, giraffes, elephants, antelopes, and even white rhinos, gathered to lick minerals essential for health. The park expands from East of Jur River, to beyond east of Jel River, 7,800 square miles in size. I said to myself, if only northern Sudanese knew the land of abundance southern Sudan was, war would rage on to eternity. Praise be to "hubris"; northerners were of the mind southern Sudan was a burden they were better off disowning. Their only fear was, should they let southern Sudan go, it would fall into the arms of Christian missionaries.

As a movement, we operated without borders in defiance of the country's laws and regulations. I do not know if by 1965, government still had people to guard the forest. If they did, we did not care to know. So, we entered the forbidding forest anyway. It was intimidating not only to the sight, all about it spoke, smelled, and felt danger was lurking here; maybe, there- anywhere! We were in numbers; therein, we each found courage and strength. I was not all the time mentally gathered to remember the details of the walk through the wild, but we did eventually emerge from that dark forest. I felt relieved.

What Sank Adhal?

Habitually taciturn faces carried thin smiles, but not wide enough to brighten the long journey ahead. We were at long last, in Bahr el Ghazal region, home, but not quite.

We were relieved now that we were no more hemmed in by gigantic trees. This time around, we shared the vast land with white rhinos (very few), giraffes, buffaloes, and other species yet we felt safer than when we were in the jungle. Some among us were familiar with the area. Still, we were careful not to disturb villages preferring instead to trot the wild till we arrived where we felt safe.

All went well till we came to the Jur River. It must have been around June or thereabout,1966. The river was tempestuous as it looked formidable. Nonetheless, we had to cross.

We had no boats, not trained to innovate and quick to act without weighing the consequences. All these shortcomings, sins of woeful unpreparedness, would become manifest in the way we crossed Jur River. The first to jump into the river were the enthusiasts. They had mighty tussles with the waves but safely made it to the other bank. The show of power went viral: I almost threw myself into the jaws of the raging waves, but someone grabbed me timely. I do not recall his name, but I owe him my life. Many followed the act; they too crossed safely to the other side. I watched waves after waves of men challenge nature and emerged successful.

Then, before my turn came among the three last to cross, another batch jumped into the water, among them, Adhal, a huge man strewn with muscles, so powerful he could slap the waves flat and walk with ease on to the other side. It was him nature chose to offer to the river gods. As expected, he swam like hippopotamus, from time to time raising his head to take in air. In a short while, he was a few feet away from the other side.

Then, momentarily, he appeared stalled; uttered a loud cry, and went under; then reappeared three times in succession; then, no more was seen of him again. Half hour later, a giant turtle petered its head out as if to let us know it was the predator. Indeed, we all concluded it was it that claimed the life of our comrade and brother.

Now that I know better, it was unlikely the turtle was the culprit. Turtles are known to pull their victims right to the bottom of the river and lie on them for days until the body rots and are now able to eat up their victim's rotten and loosen flesh. The appearance of the turtle must therefore have been coincidental, probably disturbed by the swimmers and whatever sunk Adhal.

The river is known to be home to hundreds of thousands of crocodiles and hippopotami. But, if a hippo were the killer, it would have made visible show of the kill, tearing through the water like a mad bull.

Chances are that it was a crocodile that took our comrade in arms, Adhal. While they hibernate in their dry holes in the three months of dry season, they would emerge very hungry when rains increased and the rivers filled up, flooding their underground holes. At such times, crocodiles are known locally to be extremely dangerous, attacking land animals and humans at any opportunity. Such was the time; and it would be reasonable to assume a crocodile took our formidable brother.

They say necessity is the mother of invention. After the incident, we cut down some trees and made a raft out of it making sure it was sturdy enough to take three of us and the few arms we had. We made it not because we were stronger than Adhal; it is nature's call to preserve whom it will and dispose of others who, in our estimation, should be last to succumb.

VII

NEW BEGINNING, SAME STRUGGLE

We added comrade Adhal, commander Nyiel Abot and Fabio Deng Akol, to our individual archives of memories to keep. We marched forth as we had to when we fled Lirangu. Now we have learned from Jur River that, when duty-bound, speed on, no matter what. With that, she rushed to pour her content into the White Nile. Now, we too could not stagnate and sulk in one place. We had destinations to reach, other Anya-Nya forces to merge with and a promise to fulfill; come what may, as one, we will contribute to shielding the dignity of our people from further abuses.

Invigorated, with sturdy steps, we marched forth on our way to northern Bahr el Ghazal Province. Last year, our camp had spent nearly three weeks around Tonj area. Although I was not familiar with the surrounding, the more distance we covered, the more

I could see environing scenes that reminded me of the location where Christopher Akonon Mithiang was in command of a huge, well-armed Anya-Nya base. And indeed, those familiar with the area soon confirmed I was right.

The location of the camp was edged in my memory for reasons, one of which was close to home. It was here August last year (1965), that I ran into two of my cousins, Kuolchol Alor Kuol[20] and Nicola Adol Mithiang Miyan[21] who broke the news that our Uncle, Lewis Nyok Kuol Arop who lived in Tonj, was shot dead that morning in his bedroom in front of his wife and daughters by attackers who wore military uniforms and spoke Arabic. They also informed they feared three other relatives besides Lewis, may also have been killed.

Five adolescent young men lived with Lewis Nyok: Kuolchol Alor and Nicola Adol, in addition to Alor Kwaja[22], Manyit Daw Alei[23], and Deng Mijak Kuol[24]. Government security in Tonj was known for heightened surveillance. They kept track of who lived with whom in southern towns. They knew exactly how many people were in Lewis Nyok's house that morning and they came prepared to kill them all, six males in total. Earlier, soldiers had taken a round in town and had killed six men already. This was a little reported incident in which government of the Sudan targeted Southern intellectuals. Most victims were educators who, even with the expulsion of Missionaries from Southern Sudan, would run schools and perpetuate education among the population. It was apparently the government's plan to clear the way for Islamic education in Southern Sudan. As fall back, should southerners resist proselytization through Islamic education, government plan was to abandon them to illiteracy till they surrender to Islamic education.

Lewis' house was the last in the list of homes soldiers came to weed of male inhabitants that morning. But miracles do happen. In the end, the five boys miraculously escaped. Dinka people have a saying, "God separates things that must happen from those that are not meant to be." Only two sustained non-lethal wounds. Three hid in a bathroom outside the house, close to attackers, yet escaped unscathed in a moment reminiscent of my Lirangu encounter with my Zande savior. This time, the hero was a man from the Nubba mountains, a northern soldier who came to kill but ended up savior. What moved him to risk his life in that way, I would understand better many years later when the Nubba people would join southern Sudanese in the war against Khartoum.

Here was how future pulled a miracle off her sleeves. The Nubba man was commanded to check the bathroom where the boys were hiding. He opened the window and found them cowering in the corners paralyzed by fear. He quietly urged them not to make moves that would betray their presence. Quietly, he retreated.

With a straight face and sure foot, he joined his group. A few minutes later, the boys heard soldiers' footsteps, marching past the bathroom where they were hold up and out of the compound. They had a close shave with death, salute the selfless Nubba soldier who endangered his life to save children he came to kill.

Lewis Nyok was one of the earliest champions of education in Southern Sudan, an educator whose efforts have thus far been overlooked even by researchers who have gathered wealth of information on him over the years. Ngok of Abyei is yet to publicly credit Nyok Kuol for being the first Ngok intellectual to stand against efforts, including by members of his family, to permanently annex the area to northern Sudan. Till his murder in August 1965, it was his unwavering position Ngok was part of southern Sudan. Decades into the future, every passing year has spoken of the acuity of his foresight; community's leadership slaughtered, cattle driven away, villagers killed, and villages burned down; even children taken to slavery. No matter what happens, Abyei has remained part of the Sudan, the very dispensation that has for decades sought to destroy the population.

My cousins also informed that before troops came for Lewis, they had already slaughtered six other men in their homes. Bodies of the deceased were hurriedly and irreverently dumped in a pit dug for the purpose well before execution. The soldiers however, retained the body of Bona Bol. The reason was as inexplicable as it was evil: Bol was endowed with a beard so bushy it would be waste, they thought, to bury him with such a priced item on his chin. They wanted to desecrate his body first. According to an eyewitness, a daughter of one of the victims present during the murder, Bol's beard was skinned off his face before he was thrown into the pit along with six others.

I have asked and continue to find answers for such brutality, was it out of hatred or something more systemic, inhuman, and degrading? Years later, I would find deeper implication to that seemingly mindless action. To be fair, still I would not dismiss the act may also have been an isolated expression of hatred for southern people, totally divorced of cultural or religious underpinnings. But history would restrain us from settling for such easy conclusions. There are documented reports in Arab/history when shaving beards off men's faces was a recognized instrument of persecution and an accepted judicial sentence for offenders the system deemed fit to humiliate. Arab conquerors of Egypt for instance, reportedly punished and shamed Egyptian men by sentencing them to beardlessness, a life of facial nudity. In the context, no punishment could be more degrading.

Perplexing, but perhaps that might have been their way of cutting down on lowlings intent on snaking their way up the ranks of bearded Arab gentry.

The question remains, was an ordinary, illiterate Sudanese soldier serving in Tonj, a remote region of the Sudan, aware of Arab infatuation with beards? Was the author of the idea an Arab in the first place? There is no denying the allure of hyper masculinity remains visible in today's Arab world. In places several degrees removed from both context and Arab roots, Sudan for example, the culture exists but in pockets.

In some parts of Sudan, beard is taken at face value as an external manifestation of virility and piety, but when the bearded person happens to be non-Muslim, the overzealous are confused about what to make of it. A beard in the face of an infidel is a riddle difficult to square with its association with piety. Perhaps, the originator of the idea to skin the beard off the late man's face, was one such devotee. I entertain doubts a soldier in such context would be privy to esoteric information on beard in Arab and Islamic culture. Bol's case stands out as a glaring testimony of why Southern Sudanese had to reject northern domination and to seek restoration of their dignity through armed struggle.

Those were the thoughts that jammed my mind as we passed by the location where Akonon Mithiang's camp was in 1965. We continued our journey north. Around Gagrial, we stopped for a short while in commander Kuol Amom's camp[25]. Some of our colleagues stayed there. The rest, including me, headed north, to Twic area, where my affiliation with Anya-Nya began.

On the way, we passed by areas that awakened strong memories in me. I remembered Ngeny Ater[26] and Bol Arop Diu[27] whom I had been with that night but in the morning, on their way on a mission, they sauntered into an ambush laid by northern army in Twic, Thon area.

I recalled heroes among them: Macham Atem, Kuol Arop Kor[28], Doldol Nyang[29], Deng Biong Mading[30] and Arop Deng Majok[31]. I particularly remember Biong Bol Wounbiong[32] who educated and provided explanations to why we roamed the wilderness away from our homes and towns where Northerners were in control. I witnessed brutalities our people had suffered but could not situate what I saw in a wider, more comprehensive context. He spoke to me about international politics, the West v. Communist East blocks; told me stories about the Czechoslovak leader, Alexander Dubcek, whom he loved; spoke of the tyranny of Franco of Spain and the plot by the Arab world to stand with Arabicized Sudan to Islamize and Arabize Southern Sudan or, failure to, depopulate it altogether.

We arrived in Twic, Adiang area, a few miles away from my home, Mijak Manyuar. One midnight, Kuol Arop Kor, an uncle from my mother's side, a senior officer, tied my hands and feet so fast I had no time to fight back. He carried me on his back and repeatedly kept saying: "it is time you returned to school". After some distance, he untied my feet making sure I did not run away as we approached my family's home in Mijak Mannyouar.

He had to drop me there before daybreak lest he be sighted, and his presence reported to army headquarters in Abyei. When we arrived home, to ensure I would not take to the bush after him, he once again tied my feet and hands, gagged my mouth, and left me right at the center of my father's compound. His task was accomplished. My physical association with Anya-Nya was thus terminated. At daybreak, when people came out of the rooms, there I was after two years of absence.

As I was about to be reintroduced to the very context I had consciously disavowed, I knew my new beginning would be a continuation of how I felt since the day I appeared with my father before the school admission board nearly six years earlier. The two incidents, Elmuglad and the burning of Ngok region, only came to confirm something was fundamentally flawed with the relations between northern and southern Sudanese.

One thing was clear, Anya-Nya was only but a chapter in a book that had an introduction a conclusion; sandwiched in between, a vast array of experiences weaved together by one theme, the strife for enduring freedom, a power second only to everlasting freedom which comes with death.

Notes

1. Christopher Akonon Mithiang: Akonon was killed in or about the end of 1966. He will be remembered for the combats he waged in and around Rumbek and Tonj.

2. Abyei: Abyei is presented in a shocking way on google earth. The first picture that appears is of Arab cattle leisurely grazing alongside Nyamoura River. When the camera zooms into Abyei Town, the crescent is first to display; then, "Abyei Grand Mosque". On three counts, Abyei and the entire area is presented as northern and Arab town. Indigenous population, the Ngok, and their cattle, do not feature; if in some subtle ways they do, it must be in fine print, not meant for all eyes to see. I read it as the tip of a huge scheme which, if ever detected and taken seriously, may come too late to mend.

   This alone, is enough suggestion Abyei has not moved an inch from where it was in 1965. It remains a land at the mercy of Sudan and proxies, the Arab tribes whose life long wish had been to level Abyei to the ground as many times as it takes to break the will of the population and force them to flee the land.

   The reasons for which I rebelled, and many did in 1965, are still there and more pronounced. Today, two kinds of people live in Abyei, eyeing one another like roosters locked in an existential fight: desperados, out to make a huge living at any cost, and their nemesis, the hotheads, who would not abandon Abyei come what may.

3. Captain Minyang Apaie: I learned he turned himself in to Abyei Sudanese Armed forces shortly after I left the area for the trip to the Congo. Much as I tried, I could not get information as to how he, a much respected commander, gave up the struggle with such ease. We cannot opine as he must have had his profound reasons for doing so.

4. Lieutenant Macham Atem: I met Macham Atem in 2011 in a meeting organized by Ngok and Twic intellectuals. The Topic was inherently divisive: determination of borders separating the two communities. Presenters on both sides of the artificial divide went mercilessly after one another not mindful of long term consequences on the two communities. Then an elderly gentleman from Twic side spoke. His tone was the voice of reason, I thought. It rang well above the conflicted echo chambers in which we were locked to speak of eternal ties between the two communities. He sounded

spiritual, a man above minutia. That man was Macham Atem, the vibrant officer with whom I was the morning Ngeny Ater and Bol Arop Dieu from Ngok were killed in an ambush in 1965 by northern troops in Twic Thon area. If the two communities had own sons to die together to liberate Southern Sudan, they can come together, create a cause for which they can live together in harmony.

5. Kerubino Atar: He was killed in combat sometime in 1966. I could not gather insights to the circumstances surrounding his heroic demise.

6. Paul Mayiel: Was killed in combat two years after my return from the Congo. He was a ball of passion that burned for the liberation of Southern Sudan.

7. Moses, the Trumpeter: I wish I had known his full name, but he was an inspiration. To me, even I were to know his name, no name would sound more endearing than the "Trumpet" as his last name. He was a mobile public information system. I could not find any information of what became of him. The majority of people who might know have long since died.

8. Alier: Unfortunately, like Moses, I never knew his second name, but I was told he was killed heroically in combat sometime in 1966.

9. Lieutenant Kuot Mayan: Kuot, my mentor, survived the Anya-Nya war and was absorbed a prison's warden in Wau following the conclusion of Addis Ababa Peace Accord in 1972. In 1976, I had the opportunity to visit with him in his Wau house. Ten years had passed since our trip to Niangara and back. That was the last time I heard of him. Dead or alive, I hold fond memories of him to this day.

10. Lirangu: it has since remained a collection of small villages sporadically spread in the woods. However, some United Nations peace-keeping troops are in the area.

11. Captain Nyiel Abot: As narrated, he was killed that treacherous April morning. He was an intellectual of stature among most of his equals at the time. He died a young person who, given his education, would have contributed a great deal to the struggle for freedom.

12. Lieutenant Fabio Deng: he died alongside his senior, Captain Nyiel Abot, He was well educated and great public speaker. I was, in Anya-Naya speak, a Banjoz, (a little warrior), so I cannot claim to have interacted with him that closely. Fabio Deng Akol and Captain Nyiel Abot formed a powerful team.

13. Kerubino Kuanyin Bol: Perhaps of all names mention here, Kerubino had featured the most in written and oral history of the struggle for the liberation of Southern

Sudan. His valor in warfare could not be gainsaid by friend and foe alike. As to loyalty, his was never engraved in stone. It is difficult to restate his complex moves. I opine, if chartered in a graph form, it would read as this: in...out, back in, to the fold, then...the end. The last leg of his winding journey was the final break with the Sudan People's Liberation Army (SPLA), a movement he helped start in 1983 and for which he became one of its top commanders. His last brush with the leadership of the movement reportedly forced him to take refuge in Kenya.

Even there, a foreign country, his home was attacked by people believed to have been aiming to end his life. He escaped, but instead of seeking a safer place to hide, he returned to Southern Sudan where unknown gunmen, probably one of the splinter SPLA factions, spotted, killed, and buried him in a place which has not thus far been identified. Many believe it must have been somewhere at the Kenya borders. This report is strictly hearsay and should not be quoted as reliable piece of information.

14 Ayok Dengabot: He was my protector for two reasons. He was my first cousin so, although I was keen to be respected as my own man, still he took upon himself the responsibility of looking after my safety. One night, a herd of stampeding animals ran into where we were resting for the night. In a second, Ayok Dengabot rushed to my protection. Back to back with him, he told me to keep running. Whatever it was coming our way, if enemies, he would engage them with his automatic rifle. It turned out, it was a herd of buffalos on the run from something, perhaps a pride of lions. We spent the night in a state of high alert till daybreak.

The second reason was far from personal relationship I had with him. He knew something I did know. It was that thing which he felt duty bound to protect. Unbeknownst to me, I was the movement's chest. This, I believe, he knew but chose never to broach a word throughout the length of the journey. He silently protected me and whatever my back was pregnant with.

Ayok Dengabot was killed shortly before Addis Ababa Accord came to effect in 1972. He had reportedly fallen into an ambush laid by an isolated pocket of Zande tribesmen who might as well have been Zande nationals of the Central Africa Republic somewhere around River Li Yubu.

15 Elia Duang Arop: He died in 1985 a highly respected politician. We met again in 1977, eleven years after Lirangu Camp.

16 Jacob Buok Madut: I met him again in 1977. He told me he had

joined the University of Monrovia, Liberia, where he read for Bachelor of Medicine. We did not meet again, but I have been told he currently lives in the United States of America

17 Robert Mayouk Deng: I met Robert Mayouk at Juba airport shortly before South Sudan was declared independent in 2011. Even as 46 years had passed since our days in Lirangu, I could still recognize him. It took him sometime to figure out who I was, but no sooner I mentioned Lirangu, immediately, he called me by my first name. Not long after we met, I heard the news of his demise. I will always remember him for his sense of humor even during bleak hours.

18 Thomas Dhel Thiel: I have not been able to collect information on Thomas Del Thiel nor have I met him after Niangara and Lirangu. I however know he was absorbed in the Sudanese Armed Forces after the Addis Ababa Accord. He died a high ranking officer in the army.

19 Niangara: Google Earth of Niangara reveals a town frozen in time. It appears as it did in 1966: one dirt road connecting east and west of the town; a long road from the borders with southern Sudan, tired, yet resolved to meander its way across the ages to meet Uele River in Niangara; a bridge connects north and south of the town followed by a short strip of road which runs into the long, lone, dirt road mentioned above.

That is precisely how Niangara was back then. That is how it appears on Google earth in 2020, 55 years later. I could recognize the location of the catholic church and even the neighborhood where we lived. A little zeroing in and, who knows, the makeshift restaurant where we ate fish may still be there serving, heaven knows what half a century later. Where is the intentional generation of liberated Congolese I had dreamed so much about? When will they come to lift this gem of land Niangara was, and perhaps, still is?

It was not my design to contrast the fate of Abyei and Niangara, but similarities are striking at least in one regard, the need for a generation to take responsibility of liberating their lands from chains, visible and invisible. For Abyei, a generation capable of seeing through misleading alternative claims Abyei's history had been one of peaceful coexistence with neighboring Arab tribes to demonstrate, instead, it has been one uninterrupted episode of unconscionable oppression.

20 Kuolchol Alor Kuol: He went on to do great things as Sudan's ambassador to many countries and South Sudan's following independence. Geneva was his last diplomatic mission before he died suddenly on December 25, 2018. Ambassador Kuolchol Alor Kuol lived a personification of integrity, a person, in my

estimation, made of the kind of clay from which decent societies are forged. His last word in a party to which he was invited by his junior diplomats, Ambassador Kuolchol delivered a passionate plea urging leaders to allow reason to prevail as South Sudan takes a detour to a slippery slope from which recovery may prove a monumental challenge. That was his last word, some advice to the willing.

21 Nicola Adol Mithiang: he returned to the country after Addis Peace Accord in 1972, joined school and became a bank officer. He progressed in the ranks. He died in 2014, a senior officer in one of South Sudan's banks.

22 Alor Kwaja Kuol: he barely escaped death. He was shot in the jaws but, through a combination of God's mercy and will to live, Alor is alive today and occupies a high position in Abyei Regional Ministry of Education.

23 Manyit Daw Alei: He became an administrative officer in the Department of Social Welfare. He died in 1979 of food poisoning in Kadugli, Nubba Mountains. No autopsy was carried out, but his wife says Manyit was poisoned by northern secret services in the city. The Second half of 1970's was, perhaps, one of the most violent episodes in the checkered history of relationship between the people of Abyei and government proxies in Southern Kordofan Province.

24 Deng Mijak Kuol: He graduated from the University of Khartoum an engineer; practiced engineering for many years after which he joined the Sudanese army as a senior officer. He died in London in 2004, a fulfilled man.

25 Kuol Amom: I met Commander Kuol Amom in 1976, nearly 10 years after I returned home to pursue my education. He died sometime in 1980's; unfortunately, I was not lucky to gather information on the circumstances surrounding his death

26 Ngeny Ater: I have not been able to gather information on Ngeny, but I will always remember the night we all convened in his house to prepare for an encounter with advancing convoy of norther troops on the way east to where we were. Early in the morning, our troops led by Ngeny, travelled to Twic Thon to meet them. Alas, we were misinformed. Northern troop were already on the ground dug in, waiting for Anyanya to come. That was how we lost Ngeny and Bol Arop Dieu.

27 Bol Arop Dieu: He died at a young age in the same ambush in which Ngeny Ater was killed. Bol Arop Dieu was, in many ways, an exception among his peers in Ngok area. He could read and write, a skill which was uncommon among his age group. He loved education so much he read whatever piece of paper he caught sight of on the

28 Kuol Arop Kor: He was absorbed an officer in the Sudanese Games Department after Addis Ababa Agreement. I owe him thanks for forcing me to pursue my education, a foresight that had saved me in innumerable ways

29 Doldol Nyang: I met him in Juba in 2013. He looked the warrior he had always been, daring in every sense of the word. He was among the first in Ngok area to join the SPLA in 1983 upon its establishment. Doldol Nyang never went to school, but for that, he would no doubt rank among the greatest generals South Sudan ever had.

30 Deng Biongmading Kuol: He died in 2017, a high ranking officer in the SPLA police force. Deng arguably valued freedom over anything else. He was among the first in Abyei area to join Anya-Nya. When Addis Peace Accord was dishonored by the north, he was once again among the first in the area to join the SPLA. Since 1940's his life had been about scouting for opportunities to face up to northern repeated aggression against his people, the Ngok Dinka of Abyei. He died a largely unused encyclopedia of knowledge about what has kept Abyei in the north till his death.

31 Arop Deng Majok: He returned to Abyei shortly after I left for the Congo. He became a member of the Kordofan Regional assembly, a position he held till he died, reportedly, in 1979. Although he was back in the north, he never lost vision of why he joined the movement. I had the opportunity to reminisce with him about our experiences in the bush. I felt he did not regret any moment of it, if anything, he cherished it greatly.

32 Biong Bol Wounbiong: Some years ago, I was informed he was here in the Unites States for treatment. I found his number and contacted him. We had not met since we parted in 1965 but when I reminded him of our days in the bush, immediately we clicked. Biong was vastly knowledgeable. He was glued to the BBC World Service following world news. He spoke impeccable English and Arabic. I gained a lot in the few months we had spent together.

www.ingramcontent.com/pod-product-compliance
Lightning Source LLC
Chambersburg PA
CBHW030303010526
44107CB00053B/1804